W9-BXX-254

LIGHTNING
BOLT
BOOKS™

Formula One Race Cars

on the Move

Janet Piehl

Lerner Publications Company
Minneapolis

To my parents,
Ann and Rich

Special thanks to Dan Knutson,
Formula One journalist

Lerner Publications Company
A division of Lerner Publishing Group, Inc.
241 First Avenue North
Minneapolis, MN 55401 U.S.A.

Website address: www.lernerbooks.com

Library of Congress Cataloging-in-Publication Data

Piehl, Janet.
    Formula one race cars on the move / by Janet Piehl.
        p.   cm. — (Lightning bolt books™—Vroom-Vroom)
    Includes index.
    ISBN 978-0-7613-3920-5 (lib. bdg. : alk. paper)
    1. Formula One automobiles—Juvenile literature. 2. Automobile racing—Juvenile literature.
    I. Title.
    TL236P52723 2011
    796.72—dc22   2009039745

Manufactured in the United States of America
1 — BP — 7/15/10

Contents

A Special Formula

ZOOM!
This car moves fast!

This is a Formula One car.
What is a Formula One car?

A Formula One car is a kind of race car. It is built to be light and to race very quickly.

Who builds a Formula One car?

These guys work together to build a Formula One car.

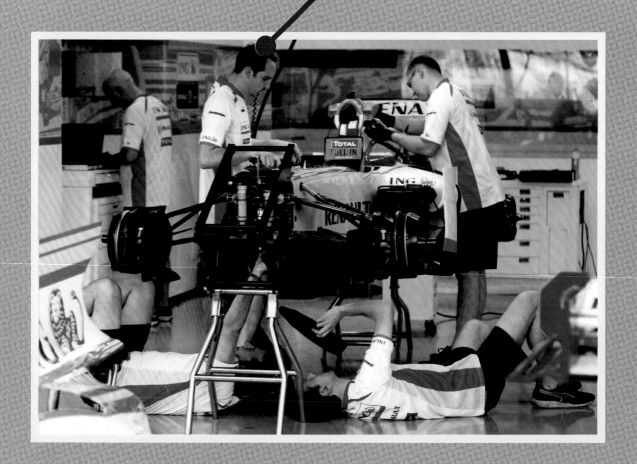

A team builds a Formula One car. The team also plans, fixes, and drives Formula One cars.

The drivers of this Formula One car take the cover off the finished car.

The team has to follow a set of rules to build the car. The set of rules is called a formula. The formula for these cars is called Formula One.

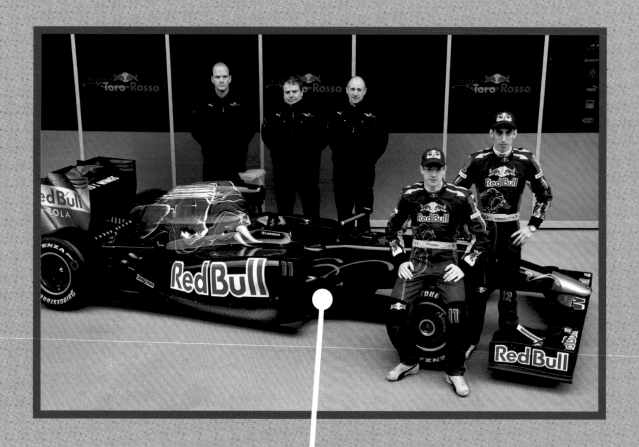

This team poses for a picture with their car. They're ready for a race!

Formula One Ingredients

The team puts a powerful engine in the car. The engine makes the car go very fast.

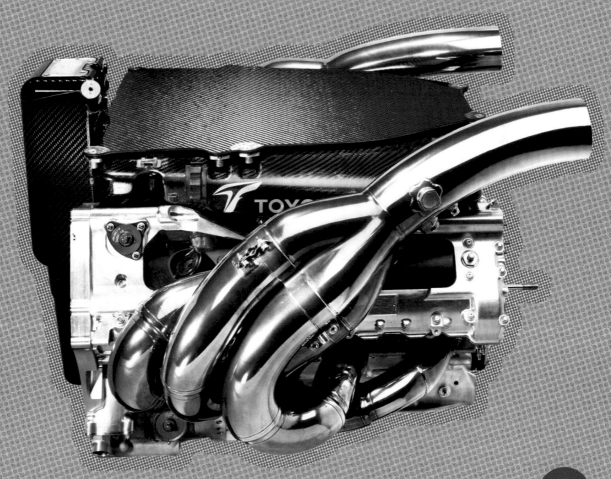

The engine sits in back of the car.

This is the car's powerful engine.

The suspension connects the wheels to the car.

The car's suspension helps it go around curves and over bumps.

The bodywork covers the engine. It is smooth so the car can zoom down the track.

Members of a Formula One team check over part of the bodywork.

A Formula One car has wings. The wings are on the front and the back of the car. Do the wings help the car fly?

The wings on the front and the back of a Formula One car don't flap!

No! They keep the car on the ground. Air moves over the wings and pushes them down. The wings keep the car from tipping over.

The wings on lightweight Formula One cars allow them to go super fast and stay close to the ground.

The Grand Race

Today is race day! A Formula One race is called a Grand Prix. The team gets the car ready to race.

The team rolls out the car on race day.

The driver gets into the car. The driver sits in the cockpit. Only one person can ride in the cockpit.

The steering wheel and other important controls are in the cockpit.

The steering wheel of a Formula One car has built-in controls.

The cars line up. Off they go! ZOOM! They start to speed around the track.

The track is curved. The cars must slow down to go around a curve.

Cars wind around bends in the track.

ZOOM! The track is straight. The cars go very fast. Special tires help the car grip the track.

The Safety Formula

SMASH! Oh no!
This car has had an accident.
Is the driver hurt?

This car crashes during a race.

No. The driver's car protected him. He wears a helmet and a seat belt. His clothes keep him safe from fire.

This driver's helmet protected him during a crash.

22

Why has this car stopped?

It needs more gas to make it go. It has gone to the pit. It is making a pit stop.

A car makes a pit stop during a race.

23

The team in the pit gives the car more gas. The team also changes the car's tires. ZOOM! The car flies off to finish the race.

The car speeds away from the pit. It's time to race again!

The race is almost done. This car passes another. The driver wants to get ahead. Who will win the Grand Prix?

Look! Two cars finish the race. Which one finished first?

This driver
and his team
have the
fastest car.
They win
the grand
prize!

Formula One Diagram

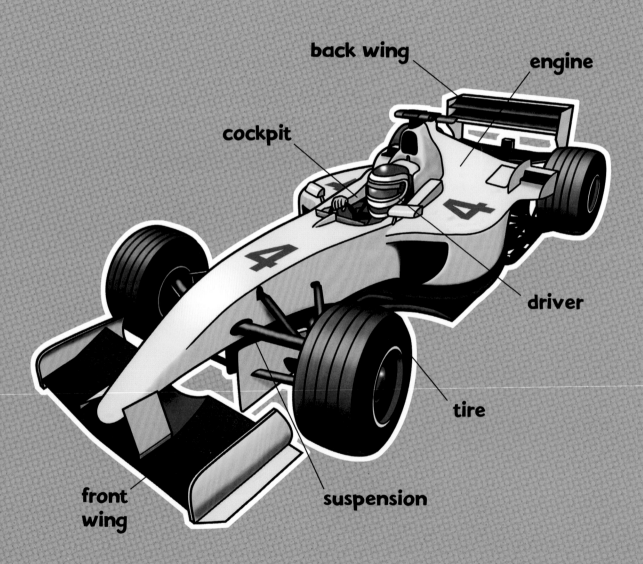

back wing

engine

cockpit

driver

tire

front wing

suspension

Fun Facts

- Grand Prix races are about 190 miles (306 kilometers) long. That is the distance between New York City, New York, and Baltimore, Maryland. The races must stop after two hours.

- Formula One cars drive at about 200 miles (322 km) per hour during races. Regular cars drive about 55 miles (89 km) per hour on the highway.

- Twenty cars race in a Grand Prix.

- Drivers want to make pit stops as fast as possible. Some pit stops are only five seconds long!

Glossary

bodywork: the smooth part of a Formula One car that covers the car's engine

cockpit: the place where the driver sits in a Formula One car

engine: the part that gives the car power to move

Grand Prix: French for "Grand Prize." Grand Prix is the name for a Formula One race.

pit: an area next to the track where a driver can stop to get gas, change tires, and make repairs

suspension: the part of a Formula One car that connects the wheels to the main part of the car

wings: parts on the front and back of a Formula One car that keep the car from tipping over

Further Reading

Brecke, Nicole, and Patricia M. Stockland. *Cars, Trucks, and Motorcycles You Can Draw.* Minneapolis: Millbrook Press, 2010.

Collision Kids
http://www.collisionkids.org

Floca, Brian. *The Racecar Alphabet.* New York: Atheneum Books for Young Readers, 2003.

Gunn, Richard. *Racing Cars.* Milwaukee: Gareth Stevens, 2007.

Morganelli, Adrianna. *Formula One.* New York: Crabtree, 2007.

The Official Formula One Website
http://www.formula1.com

Index

Photo Acknowledgments

The images in this book are used with the permission of: © Mark Thompson/Getty Images, pp. 1, 16, 18, 23, 24; AP Photo/Gero Breloer, pp. 2, 12; © Rajesh Jantilal/Africa Media Online/Alamy, p. 4; AP Photo/Alberto Pellaschiar, pp. 5, 31; AP Photo/Mark Baker, pp. 6, 27; © Jasper Juinen/Getty Images, pp. 7, 8; © Toyota via Getty Images, p. 9; © Stuart Franklin/Getty Images, p. 10; © Force India F1 via Getty Images, pp. 11, 13; © Clive Rose/Getty Images, pp. 14, 30; © Orlando Kissner/AFP/Getty Images, p. 15; © Ferrari via Getty Images, p. 17; AP Photo/Vincent Thian, p. 19; © Vladimir Rys/Bongarts/Getty Images, p. 20; AP Photo/MTI, p. 21; © Denis Charlet/AFP/Getty Images, p. 22; © Mike Hewitt/Getty Images, p. 25; © Formula One/1™/Artemis Images, p. 26; © Laura Westlund/Independent Picture Service, p. 28.

Front cover: © Mark Thompson/Getty Images (both).